Moulting Days

AF373520

e k a
PUBLISHING

LIFE AFTER UNIFORM
ANTHOLOGY

Moulting *Days*

LIFE AFTER UNIFORM

Anthology of stories/essays/memoirs on the difficulties faced by retiring soldiers transiting to civilian life

Indian Armed Forces are highly trained and ready to respond at a moment's notice to human-made or natural disasters anywhere in the country or outside. While in service, our armed forces dedicate their lives, and their families' lives, to military service. Yet when it comes to life after retirement, they face lot of challenges in the society. With both imaginary and real stories, we would like to highlight this serious topic with light hearted and creative stories from imagination from the authors. The author and publisher have made every effort to ensure that the information in this book is well within the creative freedom and the intention is not to harm anyone's emotion.

This is a work of fiction. Names, characters, businesses, places, events, locales, and incidents are either the products of the author's imagination or used in a fictitious manner. Any resemblance to actual persons, living or dead, or actual events is purely coincidental.

All rights reserved. No part of this publication may be reproduced, stored in a retrieval system, or transmitted, in any form or by any means, electronic, mechanical, photocopying, recording or otherwise without the prior permission of Eka Publishers.

First Published in India by Eka Publishers 2021
Copyright © Eka Publishers

Moulting Days
Editor: Smriti
Cover: Aniruddh Vaidya
FICTION + NON FICTION

Authors:
Anil Kumar Jaswal
Ashish Khandare
Deesha Soni
Dr Surya Kaladhar
Hari Arayammakul
Kaweri Mishra
Mridul C Mrinal
Rabi Chatterjee
Rajeev A. Masih
Saheli Banerji
Swapnil Saurav

EKA PUBLISHERS
#118 Ushodaya Enclave, PO Miyapur
Hyderabad 500049. INDIA
ekapresshyderabad@gmail.com
+91 8008-101-590
www.ekapress.org

FOREWARD

Retirement to most of us is a permanent break from our routine job or work. We are stressed out in our work lives and dream of retirement. We plan exotic holidays and a carefree life ahead. Just imagine, a whole stretch of time hanging loose on our hands, which we firmly believe that we would use to the best of our ability, in hobbies like reading, gardening or cooking! God knows what each one does after retirement. But the general feeling of a retired person is one of leisure and time spent meaningfully.

For army men, however, retirement is the beginning of a new life. They will have to shed their military overalls for the life of a civilian. Until then, every minute is precious. It is a perpetual question of life and death. Their entire day is spent either in training for the tough times or on duty at the borders, keeping vigil 24x7. And when called to wage wars, they are prepared to lay down their lives unquestioningly, for the safety of their countrymen. They retire young, like say when they are in their mid-thirties. After this, they don't have to be ever alert or active. But they have the potential to lead a healthy and prosperous life of a civilian.

Retirement for army men means making up for the lost time with family and friends. Later, it is taking up some job or avocation, to spend their time usefully. But the change, from a highly disciplined, active lifestyle, to one in which they have practically nothing to do, is overwhelming for these bravados. Some are sad, others are confused. Most of them are happy to go back home to their families. But soon these well-trained fighters, full with the spirit of nationality, realize that they are not in sync with the 'comfortable' lifestyles of their own family members, especially their children.

So how do they cope? Each one has a unique solution to this problem. Their stories therefore make an interesting read. With this in mind, Eka Pblishers have come up with Moulting Days, a collection of 10 short stories that speak of soldiers' paradoxical situations. These stories are inspired by a book, Monsoon Mischief, written by Hari Aryammakul, himself an ex-serviceman. The synopsis of Hari's book can be found in the Preface to this collection of short stories. Monsoon Mischief is a fictional tale of a retired soldier, who finds the challenges of civilian life a different ball game altogether.

The 10 stories in Moulting Days deal with the ways and means discovered by these bravados, to resolve the issues faced by them in civilian life. They could come to terms with a 'corrupt society' as in Life after Retirement, by Ashish Khandare, use their experiences to become a coach to young students, as in Trial of Life by Disha Soni or even take to writing books like in Pieces of Rose by Rabi Chatterjee. They could even choose the spiritual path like in 'He is a Soldier,' by Saheli Banerji or dare to fight ghosts like in Ghosts in the Walls by Swapnil Saurav.

All the stories are a variety of possibilities that are open for ex-servicemen who have to return to civilian life, after a stint in the Armed Forces. Each story is unique in that it shows how the protagonist comes to terms with life of an ordinary citizen of the land, after selfless service in a position of high honour and dignity.

-Nalini Dharanipragada, Ex-Journalist

Nalini is a retired media professional, and has worked as a sub-editor in several Hyderabad based dailies including Deccan Chronicle and the Hans India. She also worked with other media channels like ap7am.com and HMTV.

FROM THE AUTHOR OF MONSOON MISCHIEF

I am excited to know that Eka Publishers is publishing an anthology of stories/essays/memoirs on the difficulties faced by retiring soldiers transitioning to civilian life. Governments usually help homecoming soldiers to resettle by granting them special privileges. But the fine adjustments soldiers have to make to blend in with the new environment often goes unnoticed. Reconnecting with the family and community, re-establishing roles and finding new ones, adjusting with the new routines, picking up the subtle nuances in conversations and new workplace lingo, compromising with the changing values and priorities, experiencing loss of confidence and worthlessness, a feeling of lack of clarity, chaotic nature, and ambiguousness in interactions are some of the challenges usually faced by the homecoming veterans. These transitional issues are not universally equal and the intensity may vary with factors like the age of the discharged veteran and the region he belongs to. For instance, a discharged soldier from a frontline province like Punjab may feel quite at home, then the one from the peninsula. And certainly, some soldiers with better innate management skills and traits may handle the 'culture shock' more smoothly.

I consider it is a great honour for any book, let alone a fiction like Monsoon Mischief, to inspire its publisher develop further, on one of the topics the novel had dealt with, by bringing out an anthology on the subject. As an author, I feel humbled and really fortunate to become a catalyst in this pioneering attempt to unravel a homecoming soldier's little-known "secret sorrows".

Hari Arayammakul

EDITORS'S NOTE

Moulting Days is a brilliant situation created by the authors, however little, I am happy to be associated. The central theme of the book – how would the life of a man defending the country be when he doesn't need to anymore – is intriguing. Being forced out of our comfort zone and into a different lifestyle is difficult at the least and funny, scary and definitely inspiring at times. What is commendable about our armed forces is that, most of us may not even need to go through this transform once, but they have to at least twice in their life. Learning, unlearning, learning – and the whole thing repeated once again.

The book has identified some really fanciful and some possibly veracious situations that could arise in the life of a soldier. There is one common thing throughout these stories. The zeal and discipline inculcated in a soldier never leaves them.

K Smriti

TABLE OF CONTENTS

PREFACE

Monsoon Mischief Novel by Hari Arayammakul
Available worldwide on various platforms

Monsoon Mischief by Hari Arayammakul tells the story of Soorya, a homecoming soldier, after his long military service.

Can cantonment stories without wars and bloodshed be called a Military fiction? Then, "Monsoon Mischief" quite easily fits into the genre and the novel could well be the first military fiction in Indian English without war as the main subject. The novel has more in it in the form of a beautiful and memorable mid-life romantic relationship. Soorya at the end of his thirties falls in love with Varsha, a Delhi based girl, even as he is preparing for his discharge from the forces. The portrayal of the delicate and crumbling ecology of the rainy state of Kerala sandwiched between the Western Ghats and the Arabian Sea qualifies the novel as an eco-fiction. On the political front the novel portrays Kerala's highly rated communist movement through a soldier's eyes. Soorya is the pioneering soldier from a Party-Village (communist party stronghold) in the northern Kerala where till then terms like "Martyrdom, fighter, struggle and wars were always used in a proletarian and communist connotation". The story also presents a sarcastic view on the southern state's one-sided leftist cultural milieu, thus qualifying Monsoon Mischief as a political novel.

Monsoon Mischief gives an insider's account on an Indian soldier's life rather than a hackneyed and idealistic version. Life in the camp, the social life of billeted recruits, re-entry into civilian life, and a soldier's struggle to find a new identity after discharge are some of the sketches a reader encounters in the novel.

The blurb on the book says "How hard it is for a civilian to leave his or her place of comfort to a world of uncertainty and unfamiliarity to be transformed into a soldier! Then transition back from barracks to civilian life is harder". A soldier's transition from military to civil-life is like an astronaut's return journey to earth. Adjusting to the new situations and finding the right balance and rhythm of civilian life is not as easy as it might seem. One has to quickly adapt oneself to the changing environment where the rules of conduct are different. The reader quickly realizes the difficulties faced by a homecoming soldiers. The predicament faced by soldiers returning to a highly politicized, gulf-money-rich, Kerala and their hilarious responses when faced with an identity crisis, makes "Monsoon Mischief" a truly interesting read. A reader would hardly miss the lukewarm welcome meted out by a condescending, intellectually-elitist society to its former soldiers.

The nonlinear narrative style continuously shifting between the cantonments and the little rainy Malabar Village immensely enhances the readability of the novel. Clever mixing of facts and fantasies, smearing with magical realism (sparingly used in the blooming love scenes), juxtaposition of extremes like communist ways and military life, and skilful use of putting words to work (poetic language for portraying nature and military jargons used in cantonments) keeps the readers busy and engaged throughout.

Aruvikkulam, the ecologically fragile, fictional pastoral village, where Soorya grew up is actually a microcosm of Kerala. Leftism prospered in Aruvikkulam from the beginning and the influence of communist party is conspicuous in every sphere of life. The conflict between communists and the returning soldiers represents the friction between discipline and anarchy. The paradoxes a reader comes across in the story are actually the same that encounters in everyday Malayali life.

'Monsoon Mischief' has three parts. 'Abracadabra', 'Quick Change' and 'Fading Away'. The narrator is a friend and fellow soldier of Soorya, the protagonist.

The first part Abracadabra portrays the childhood of Soorya. He spent his early years at Aruvikkulam, a rainy mystic Malabar village. Aruvikkulam is a fictional triangular village, with three isosceles hills joining at each other's edges. The strange alignment of three hills is considered a geological wonder. On the west, where the northern and southern hills meet, there is a small gap between their edges through which the road, the only artery connecting the city forty miles away enters the village.

The wind, perpetually blowing in from the west through the pass and the recurring monsoon rains shape the contours of the life on the slopes. But what makes the village really extraordinary is its ability to tame contradictions and extremities. Communism and superstitions co-exist here.

When the second section 'Quick Change' begins, Soorya, in his late thirties, is preparing for his discharge from Air Force and resettlement back at home. His newfound love with Varsha, daughter of a Malayali Military Nursing Staff officer, unsettles his plans a bit. Varsha visits Kuttanad on a short stay at her mother's ancestral house on the picturesque island hamlet at Kuttanad. She meets Soorya in Kochi.

There are flashbacks of camp days and barrack life. Homecoming soldier into a highly politicized, middle-east-money-rich Kerala, faces an identity crisis. They make wild and farfetched attempts, sometimes reaching witty and farcical proportions, to get a foothold and acceptance in the society. Soorya has constructed a new house in the village spending almost all his earnings. Soon after, a passenger airplane crashes at the 'tabletop' airport in the city, overshooting the runway and falling in a gorge. The DGCA stops permission to operate wide-bodied aircraft from the city airport and the state government plans to acquire land for a new airport at Aruvikkulam, forty miles away from the city. The villagers protest against land acquisition and the government uses the carrot and stick tactics to deflate the movement. Soorya is devastated to lose his newly constructed house even as his growing affair with Varsha adds unexpected twists and turns to

● ● ●

his life and forces him to make last-minute changes to his plans. There is widespread desperation among villagers.

Varsha's Delhi friend Swathi and her family who belongs to a village near Shimoga in Karnataka are leaving for Europe. Varsha suggests that they buy the farmland in Shimoga and take up farming. Heartbroken, Soorya is among the first lot of villagers who sign the land transaction agreement with the government.

'Vanishing Act' has four surrealistic chapters. Varsha resigns her job in Delhi and reaches Aruvikkulam to travel to Shimoga. She stays with Soorya in the village for a few days before bidding a final goodbye to the village.

Buy online: https://ekapress.org/book/monsoon-mischief

STORY - I

GHOSTS IN THE WALLS

SWAPNIL SAURAV

GHOSTS IN THE WALLS

Newly minted keys jangled in Sanjay's hands as he unlocked the front door. Its hinges creaked as he pushed his way inside his childhood home. Dust swirled in the rays of the late afternoon sun, painting his mother's décor in golden light. He moved his fingers over the miniature statues of cats on the small entryway table and glanced at the pictures spanning his family's generations dotting the walls of the stairwell. He set his dark green pack on the floor and slipped another backpack off his shoulder. The ache in his back and neck eased; the pain served as a bitter reminder that his early twenties had passed decades ago, and his body no longer relished the physical punishment of labour.

Retirement would be good. He breathed deep, letting the characteristic woody smell rouse his nostalgia for a moment before heaving his bags off the floor and up the stairs. The second-to-last step creaked as it always did. Such a bittersweet thing to be back home. He crossed the hallway to the master bedroom. By now, his sister had packed away or gotten rid of most of their mother's belongings. Only the four-post bedframe, a new mattress in its plastic wrapping, and a set of new folded sheets remained. His bag thumped on the hardwood floor and he set to making the bed. Decades of military service shone through in the crisp corners and clean lines of his work. He fluffed a pillow. The second step creaked.

He hadn't heard the front door open. He peeked around the corner of his room towards the staircase. He ventured into the hallway on the balls of his feet and searched the house. He was alone. It must have been the wood settling after so much time of not being used. He resumed putting his clothes away and storing his belongings.

After dinner, he set the dirty dishes in the sink and turned on the faucet. Nothing happened. He raised a brow, and his moustache tickled his nose as he scrunched his lips. He shut the water off and tried again. Nothing. He sighed and reached for the spigot. The water sprayed out, ricocheted off the curve of a spoon, and sprayed out of the sink. He sputtered and guarded his face from the onslaught as he fumbled to close the faucet, but it kept spraying water. He ducked under the sink, found the main shut-off valve, twisted it; the water finally stopped. He wiped his face and moustache, using a paper towel to dry his glasses, then tossed the dishes in the machine. He would deal with it later. He went upstairs to change out of his wet clothes and then went outside for some therapeutic gardening.

By the time evening rolled around, the smell of trimmed grass and sweat from weeding and pruning had lifted his mood. He ate a small snack and made another attempt at washing the dishes— this time without any drama. Seemed the pipes might have just needed a bit to unclog. He ambled upstairs and started the shower. Once it had warmed, he stepped into the stream and relished in how it soothed his aching muscles. He lathered himself with soap and moved under it to rinse. The water went cold, and he shrieked as the icy rivulets stung his skin. He hopped out of the shower, slipped, yelped, and barely managed to catch himself on the counter. Fuming, he shut off the water.

Laughter echoed from the hallway.

His stomach lurched and his spine tingled. He whipped a towel around his waist, searched for a weapon, but came up empty. His gun was in the bedroom. What could he use? The toilet tank cover. He lifted the ceramic lid off and raised it to his shoulder. With a deep breath, he leaped into the hallway and yelled, brandishing his new weapon.

Empty.

"I must be more tired than I thought," he said to himself, shaking his head. He replaced the cover, finished towelling off, and went to bed. In the morning he would call a plumber and that would be the end of his problems.

***

Loud knocking startled Sanjay from his sleep, the following morning. He grumbled a curse and slid out of his bed. He shuffled to his closet to pick out a robe. Another loud pounding echoed from downstairs.

"I'm coming! Have you no patience?" He thumped down the stairs and ripped the door open. "What—Oh no."

"Yes, it's me. Don't look so upset about it, little brother." The woman with wild curly black hair streaked with silver, several necklaces with multitudes of stones, earrings of mismatched styles, a balance bracelet, and all manner of bangles made of jade and who knows what else pushed her way past him. He sneezed at the overpowering scent of tea oil and peppermint as she passed by him. Her billowing ankle-length skirt swished as she powered into the kitchen and set down a hemp bag full of food— most of it organic, and none of it anything he wanted or needed in his kitchen.

Sanjay rubbed his temples, then closed the door. He went back to the kitchen and knew better than to stop her. It would be easier to just throw it all out or donate it after she left.

"Why are you here?" he asked.

She clicked her tongue against her teeth. "You retire from the military, move into our mother's home after not seeing me for twenty years, and you expect me not to welcome you home? You really have forgotten your heart, haven't you?"

Sanjay pinched his nose. "No, I haven't. I only arrived yesterday, and you know I need time to—" The stair creaked again.

"What was that?" she asked.

"Nothing, just the house getting used to having people in it again. How did you even know I was here?"

"Oh, I come by the house regularly to renew its aura. I drove by last night and saw your car." She slammed and opened cabinets as she talked. The stair creaked again. She stopped and squinted. "You know. The energy here feels strange. I thought it was because you had shown up, but now I'm not so sure."

Sanjay sighed. "No. It's not strange. Houses don't have energy; please stop. I don't want you to—" She shushed him. She closed her eyes, grasped one of the necklaces with a huge crystal and hummed.

"You're being ridiculous. This is completely unnecessary."

She spun in a slow circle as she lifted the gem up, continuing her chant. Sanjay threw his hands up. "Why do I even try?"

"I need to do a full examination." She ran out of the house before Sanjay could stop her. He flopped backward on his chair and whispered a prayer begging for strength and fortitude. She bounded back in the room holding a wooden box. She lifted a bundle of sage and a butane lighter, ignited the plant, and then blew out the flames.

"Is this really necessary?" Sanjay asked.
"Shhh. Let me work."

• • •

"This is not work, you're— oh forget it." Sanjay set to organizing the rest of the groceries. "What is the point of cauliflower rice? Just make rice!"

If all he had to endure to get her out of his house was the stench of sage and her incoherent mumbling, then so be it. He'd suffered worse, though not by much. A shriek broke her chant, followed by rapid thumps as she hurried down the stairs. She ran up to him, pressed her face right to his nose and squinted at him.

"What in God's name are you doing?" He asked as he pulled away.

"Hmmm. I was seeing if you brought them. But... no, it seems you are clean."
"Clean?"

"Yes. You have ghosts." She licked her fingers, waved her hand in the air, and then licked them again. "Yes. Two ghosts."

Sanjay blinked at her. "Okay. You're done. Goodbye, thank you for the horrendous groceries, and for stopping by." Sanjay dumped the rest of the contents of her bag, handed it to her, and then ushered her out the door.

"Mark my words, brother! It's only going to get worse!" she yelled as he slammed the door.

* * *

He breathed a sigh of relief. He grabbed an apple and went to sit down. The leg of the chair snapped. He smacked his arm on the table and landed on his rear with a loud thump. How on Earth... It was an old chair, bound to break, and he had gained weight since his youth. Add it to the list of things to update. The stair creaked again. He picked himself up with a groan and grimace, rubbing his backside as he stood. He kicked the remnants of the chair out of the way, sat in a different one, and sneezed. Did his sister bathe in tea oil? He slid his laptop from the backpack next to table and set to work finding a plumber. Midway through his research, the internet cut out.

"Why does nothing work in this ancient house?" he groaned.

He slammed his fist on the table, rose, slipped on a puddle and growled as he stomped up the stairs. He checked the connection on the router and reset it. He went back downstairs and unlocked the laptop. A video blasted lewd sounds from the speakers. He slammed the laptop shut, but the sounds kept playing. He opened the laptop again and tried to close the window, but it didn't respond. The video kept playing and, desperate, he yanked the battery out of the laptop.

Giggles rolled in from all around. Eyes wide, Sanjay whipped his head about in search of their origin. Did he bang his head when he fell? Seconds after he heard it, the laughter stopped. A headache crawled out from the back of his skull and crept over his scalp.

• • •

"Why did she have to come here," he moaned. He lifted himself up and decided the best way to spend the rest of the night was by scouting a new running route. He dressed himself and went outside to clear his mind.

***

Sanjay threw the door open and stopped to check his Fitbit. A decent time for a new route. He flicked his shoes off, and his chest heaved as he peeled off his sweaty clothes and threw them in the laundry hamper in the bathroom. His hand stopped on the faucet knob. This was silly. It was just plumbing, there was no such thing as ghosts. He wrenched the shower on and didn't wait for the water to warm. In less than thirty seconds he was done and out. The rest of the day went by without incident. He managed his finances, checked his stock portfolio, and ate a peaceful dinner. Night came and with heavy eyelids, he set his phone on the bedside table and slid himself between his sheets. Just as he was about to cross the bridge from waking to dreaming, music blared from his phone at full volume.

He screamed, scrambled out of bed, snatched his pistol from the desk, and shot his phone. He panted, stared at the smoking bullet hole in the middle of the shattered screen. Maniacal, cackling laughter bounced off the walls. He aimed his gun at a wall, then the next, trying to pinpoint the source.

"To hell with this." He ran out of his room.

Something yanked the rug out from under him and he landed on his stomach. Not waiting to catch his breath, he scrambled up, gasping for air, and sprinted down the stairs. Pictures flew off the walls as he passed them. Laughter hounded him as he ran. He opened the front door, slammed it, and dove into his car. The tires screeched and the engine roared as he tore into the street. Next thing he knew, he was pounding on his sister's door. She opened it and took in his pajamas, dishevelled hair, wild eyes, and heaving breath.

"I told you," she said, and moved aside to let him in.
"Yes. Okay, maybe you were right. How do I get rid of them?"

"It's very simple. Tea?" She motioned to the small table in her kitchen. Surrealist paintings, sculptures of genitalia, crystal formations, woven mandalas, books on mysticism, and dream catchers adorned every inch of her living space.

Sanjay sneezed. "No. Just, tell me what to do." He pushed a stack of magazines off a chair and sat down. "My god, have you ever heard of cleaning?"

"These crystals are for cleansing, yes," she said as she pointed to an array of rocks on the sink.

"Oh for— I don't have time for this. How do I get rid of it?"

"Them. You have two ghosts, and as I mentioned, the solution is two-fold. First you must force them to show themselves."

"How am I—"

"You're a smart man. I'm sure you'll think of something. Once they have been exposed, then you must complete their unfinished business."

Sanjay sighed. He rubbed his eyes. "Do you have a blanket that doesn't reek of essential oils?"

His sister blinked. "Why wouldn't I anoint my blankets with soothing scents to help me sleep?"

"Forget it. I'll just sleep in my car."

"Such a traditionalist. Fine, but before you go, take this," she said and handed him a bag with several green crystals. "Peridot. For protection."

Sanjay thought better of rejecting the gift and put the bag in his pocket. It wasn't worth the fight, and he needed to sleep. He thanked her, went back to his car, grabbed a jacket from his trunk, and spent an uncomfortable night in the front seat.

***

Still in his pyjamas, Sanjay pushed the door to his house open. He frowned at shattered pieces of glass strewn all over the floor. These ghosts need to be gone.

"How do I get them to show themselves?" he wondered aloud as he closed the door. He scanned the kitchen, the hallway leading to the living room, the stairway, and considered the events. Water splashing him in the face, turning the hot water off in the shower, blasting pornography on his laptop, startling him with loud music...

"They're teenagers!"

He had an idea. If they really were young, then he needed to do something that youths hate. Easy. He barked a laugh, then took his clothes completely off. He started cleaning the mess completely nude. He cooked in the buff, turned on talk radio with full volume, danced and sang old songs. At one point the radio crackled and shut off, so he started doing Yoga in the living room.

"Ok, old man, we've had enough, please put some clothes on!" A wispy figure materialized in front of him. The young, boyish features grimaced and looked away while Sanjay bolted upright. A girl the same age as the boy appeared next to him.

"Do you really have to do that naked?" she asked with her face puckered up.

"I can't believe my sister was right," Sanjay whispered.
"Clothes, please?!" The ghosts pleaded in unison.
Sanjay folded his arms. "Not until I get some answers. Why are you still here? Why my house?"

"Ugh, fine," the girl said.

"We were on our way to pull off our senior prank," the boy said. "It was going to be one for the history books!"

"Yeah, too bad a drunk driver killed us right outside this house that night," the girl said. She leaned against the boy and crossed her arms.

"That's it? You wanted to pull off a prank? If I do it for you, will you leave my house?"
The boy's eyes widened, and the girl fidgeted with her school uniform.

"You, old man, would go to a high school and set off stink bombs in the ventilation system?"

Sanjay sighed and dropped his hands. How simple-minded. A stink bomb would not even be worthy of a footnote, but it made his task simple. "I was a soldier. I did many secret missions, and dropping stink bombs in an air vent would be an easy task."

The boy leaped for joy, and the girl let out a whoop.
"I've seen our payload hidden in your yard," the girl said. "It must have been thrown from the car when we got hit."

"Alright, that's a good place to start." Sanjay headed outside and the youths complained about his clothing once again.

He dressed himself and set about combing through the shrubbery near the street. He found a small box hidden in a bush

* * *

and went back inside. He held up the box, and the teens leaped for joy. Luckily, their school was a short drive away, and it was the same one he attended as a boy. He parked on the street and watched students come and go at the end of the day. Parents greeted their children, friends laughed together, and he realized that he missed that feeling. A couple walked by hand in hand and a half-smile crept up his face as he remembered his first girlfriend. He wondered where she was now.

Once all the students and the staff had gone, he went to a window with a broken latch that he had often used himself as a teen—counting it as a silver lining of poor public education budget—and snuck into the main building. He set the stink bombs on top of the grate on the floor, grabbed a handful of tissues from the teacher's desk, and stomped on the glass containers to release their foul smell. The door to the hallway opened and, as he walked down the hall, he noticed a display case with clippings of a news story and wilting flower wreaths. A tribute to the two students that died. An engraved plaque on the bottom of the case read:

Voted Prom King and Queen, we honour the memory of our two seniors.

Attached to the plaque was a photo of the two youths standing side by side wearing crowns, surrounded by paper chains, confetti, and balloons. Their bright smiles and awkward posing sent a lance of sadness through Sanjay's chest. This prank was not their final task.

When he arrived at home, he sat at his table and waited. The second hand on his wristwatch ticked. He made himself a light dinner, then stood at the sink. He turned the faucet on and dodged the stream of water that bounced off his plate.

"I know you're still here," he said. The ghosts appeared behind him and he sat back down at his table. "I completed the prank, but I didn't think you would really go." The boy sat down as well and the girl stood behind him resting her hands on his shoulders. "You two were voted Prom King and Queen, weren't you?"

The girl beamed. "We were. It was such a wonderful night."

The boy leaned back and rested his head on her forearm. "It really was. We had so much fun. I wish¬—" he stopped himself and sat up straight.

"I think I know what's really happening here," Sanjay said. He stood up and set a kettle to boil. "Tell me, were you more than friends before you died?"

"What?" the boy said. "Oh, no we were always just friends. Ever since we were children. We grew up with each other." The girl bit her lip.

"Hmm. You know, there is a benefit to being old," Sanjay said. "You learn a lot of things, lose a lot of people." His voice softened. "Leave many things unsaid." The boy cracked his knuckles, and the girl pulled at the ends of her hair, flipping it around and twisting it in her fingers. "My sister told me ages ago that words have energy. And like energy, they cannot be destroyed, only transferred. She also said energy can be both healing and destructive. As such, the words you hold have the potential to be both. Choosing which ones, you keep and which ones you share is a very important skill. I didn't believe her then." The kettle whistled. He shut off the stove and poured a measure of steaming water into a mug. "Nor did I understand what she was saying. At the time, our mother was sick, and I was still deployed." He pulled a lemon slice out of the refrigerator, squeezed in the juice, and plopped the fruit into his hot water. He sighed as he eased himself back into his chair.

"What are you getting at?" the boy asked.

"I believe the words you're keeping within yourselves are keeping you here."

The girl opened her mouth to speak but halted short of saying anything. The boy's leg bounced as his jaw worked side to side. Sanjay sipped his water. The boy stood up, his body passing through the seat.

"Ever since freshman year, after that summer I came back from camp... I saw you again and I knew that you were special. That I didn't want to spend another summer without you. I didn't say anything because I was afraid it would ruin our friendship if you didn't feel the same way. Now, I'm afraid that if I say something, we won't go on together to whatever is next. But I can't hold it in. I have loved you my entire life. I loved you as my best friend

● ● ●

when we were children, and I loved you as something more for years. I—"

The girl grasped his hands and rested her forehead on his chest. "I have wanted us to be more than friends for as long as I can remember. You were kind when others chose to be cruel. The summer you left was the summer I realized you were my rock. Even when we grew up, and we ran in different circles, you remained my closest ally. When you asked me to be your Prom date, I thought you were finally going to ask me to be your girlfriend... But even when you didn't, I was happy to go with you anyway."

"Well, will you be my girlfriend now?" he asked.
She smiled and wrapped her arms around him. "Yes."

"I love you," he whispered, and kissed the top of her head.

A pinpoint of light shone over the two, and even as they dissipated into particles of shimmering blue dust, they never let go of their eternal embrace.

Sanjay finished his drink. A heaviness weighed on his chest and laboured his breath. He stood, went to the phone hanging on the wall, and dialled his sister.

"Are they gone?" she asked in greeting.
"Yes, they're gone. Do you remember what you told me about words and energy?"

"Of course, why do you think I always tell you the truth?"

"Well, I realized I have been holding on to words I should share. I'm glad you're my sister, and I'm grateful you came over yesterday. Not just for the ghosts."
"I love you too, baby brother."

Silence hung in the air as tears threatened to spill from his eyes. He cleared his throat. "Also, I think it best to stay on your good side. The last thing I need is for my mystic sister to haunt me." His sister cackled.

STORY - II

TRUE CALLING

KAWERI MISHRA

TRUE CALLING

Rajeev retired from Indian armed force at the age of 37, he didn't have a lavish lifestyle, but he was happy that he could pursue his passion for photography. He was a widower and led a lonely but meaningful life. He always wanted to spend his retirement with his wife in his hometown but fate took her away at a very early age.

He lived in his ancestral home and rented out the ground floor of the house to a Tamil family, comprising of a young man Raghu and his mother. Though the pension from the armed force was enough for his simple life, he photographed marriages, birthdays, and other parties in his locality and made extra buck to pursue his passion further. Transitioning from the army back to civilian life wasn't easy for him especially without Roopa his wife. He used to have nightmares of fatal wars he had been a part of, woke up in cold sweats, and often felt lonely.

He partook his meals at a quiet eatery, the owner was his father's friend. The owner loved Rajeev like his own son and hence took extra care to make sure that he received proper meals. Every evening he would go for tea there and quietly occupy his favourite corner and work for hours editing his photographs.

Being an army man, he was well organized and chivalrous. He was also quite observant a characteristic of a service man.

One evening while in the café he saw a woman who was also a regular visitor to the café worried and anxious. He was captivated by the angelic modesty of this young woman from the very first day he saw her. Though they never spoke he always wanted to know more about her. He saw that the woman was disconnecting someone's call incessantly. He couldn't stop himself today and asked her if everything was alright with her. She didn't respond and left hastily. Rajeev peeped out of the café window; there he saw the woman talking to a guy who looked like a pimp. He was forcing her inside the car when she rejected, he injected something and took her away. Rajeev realized something was wrong.

He left the café and kept thinking about the incident, was his hometown under some kind of human trafficking mafia, or was there more to it. He was anxious and when next evening he again met the girl he confronted her. He wanted to know if she was in any trouble and needed his help. She said she was a prostitute and doing all this of her own accord and that she didn't need his help. Rajeev was shaken, her words caught him off guard and he didn't know how to respond. She was too young to go through all these. She was pretty and her innocence amused and charmed him. Rajeev felt that she was trying to cover something up.

Rajeev left the café and started his research on the town businesses and contacts who could help him find out what was happening. Being a local he was able to get into the right places. The owner of a photocopy and printout shop helped him reach the guy who offered the prostitute services. To his surprise, it was a dual business of drugs and prostitution. He initially thought to inform the local policeman, Mr. Gupta. But later during his investigations, he found out that Mr. Gupta was getting his sop from this business and he was ok with this illegal business.

It was a misty cold foggy night and Rajeev was walking through the streets of his hometown. He was baffled thinking that the place which meant so much to him and the one who had been dying to come back to during his entire stint at the army was now in the clasp of the mafia. His hometown had been taken over by verboten market and he could do nothing about it. He was engrossed in these thoughts and didn't notice Raghu his tenant approaching him. Raghu came to know about Rajeev's mission and was keen to join him. He had lost his close friend Vasu recently to drugs. Raghu said he knew people who sell drugs to youngsters and lure them to prostitution and drugs.

Both of them arrived at the drug peddler's place of business and pretended to be drug sellers. They reached the grey market through him. There he saw Radha the same girl whom he used to meet in a café. She was standing amongst the chippies. Her innocence covered up to look like a hooker. Rajeev could not bear the sight and just left that place. Rajeev had fallen in love with Radha and wanted to take her out of the mess at any cost. The next day he called up his army contacts and friends and spoke to them about the tricky situation in his hometown. Many of them agreed to help out and promised to reach there. Within a few days, a team was formed and a plan was chalked out on how to crack this case. With the help of an IPS officer there, these men raided the areas and recovered drugs and girls.

While everyone was busy rescuing, Rajeev was looking for Radha. He could not find her and became anxious. Radha had been tied up and put in a water tank. Rajeev got her out and could feel her very close to him. He rescued her and while conversing he got to know that she wanted to be a classical dancer and ended up here because she was cheated on by a dance troupe. Rajeev held her hand and promised her a beautiful life that she deserved.

Rajeev and Radha run an organic farming business and Rajeev is also doing a diploma course in photography. They live a quiet and peaceful life something that Rajeev had always wanted.

STORY - III

CORAL DREAMS

MRIDUL C. MRINAL

CORAL DREAMS

It was already dusk. The sinking sun poured its vibrant colours over the sky. Bilal was silent for a moment. The sight was mesmerizing. He closed his eyes. Suddenly he felt like he was no longer in this world. It was another realm. A Metaphysical realm! Where he unleashed his inner thoughts. There he met Harsimrat, His late father, brother Sadiq, Sukdev, Rajesh, Prakash and all other comrades he lost in the warfront. While he was immersed in his deep meditation, a faint breeze passed him. He opened his eyes. The night was swallowing the city. Across the backwaters, the Skyscrapers are lit up. Suddenly he realised, he was no longer in the mountains. There will not be any freezing cold nights or shelling. There will not be any sleepless nights thinking of carrying ammunition. All that kept him going on those harsh days were the thoughts of her and the boys. He is not sure to call what it is. Fate or Karma?

He no longer has those bliss that he had back then. Now, He has chosen this for them. He is sure that Harsimrat or his Kaur, Princess as he used to call her will be happy with his decision. She is watching everything from there. The ship was getting crowded. He wondered whether the boys are up from their afternoon nap. He wants them to have a peaceful childhood, to have beautiful Coral dreams! As he had in his childhood days. He wanted them away from all those hatred and conflicts. Bilal already lost the love of his life, their mother. He cannot even think of losing them too.

In his early thirties, Bilal have seen no other men have seen. He suffered enough. Whenever he thought of losing someone or something, he will look at his left leg. He still feels it. He can manage with that prosthetic leg. But, a sense of loss, a thought of incompleteness had always haunted Bilal. It was not the leg. He hardly gives any concern for it. It was Harsimrat. The naïve Punjabi girl he met in the Wagah retreating ceremony. Two weeks later, he saw her again in a busy Alley in Amritsar leading to the Harmandir Sahib. Bilal was not sure what was the feeling he had right back then. It was either affection or infatuation. Later he realised that destiny had decided for both of them to get married, make love and to have two adorable children.

Weeks later, when he was posted along the border in Mamdot, He saw the same girl in the local mandi. They came across several times. Bilal, a twenty-four-year-old young jawan did not had the courage to speak up to this young girl. His friends were playing the role of the wingmen. At last, he found some nerve to talk to her in one evening. Bilal still remembers. She was shy and her cheeks were red as apples. He was not a stranger to her. She was seeing him often from the past one month. She also had some feelings for him. Otherwise, why she is standing in front of him overflowed with shyness. Bilal's strange Hindi sounds funny to her whereas her thick Malwi dialect was quite hard to grasp for him. They often met, chatted, and had their evenings vibrant.

They come to know each other more. Still, they both had a serious thought of a martial union. The cultural rift is hard for a 20-year-old Punjabi Sikh girl and 24-year-old Muslim boy. When he had the nerve to ask for Harsimrat's hand in marriage Sukdeep, her father surprised him. He gave his consent. Faith was complex, as he never gives any hard thoughts about it. All he was believed was that everyone had a personal choice. Hameed Nallakoya, his father was schoolmaster and a visionary who thought beyond the cultural constrains of faith and beliefs. His Grandfather Nallakoya was one of the first Gandhians on the islands. He travelled to the mainland when Gandhi came to Calicut.

Bilal was often heard from his father that how Gandhiji praised the sweet Thenga Pattiri offered by his grandfather. His father however was more leaned to the progressive movements of the main land. It is said that, whatever changes happened in the main land, it will have a one-fifth effect in the islands. His father participated in several movements related to the rights of common men. Hameed Nallakoya was a social activist of Androth. He was widely known throughout the inhabited 10 islands of the archipelago. No wonder on the visionary mind of Bilal. It was indeed inherited from his father. He encouraged Bilal to pursue a career that dedicated in service of the nation. He believed that a punctual and disciplined style would give some meaning in one's life.

The marriage to Harsimrat was felt like dream come true. He never thought of a smooth transition from lovers to a wedded couple. He still remembers that day. There was no one from his side. He told his father on the phone. He knows he always had his consent. His mother with her old ways of the life was little uncomfortable with his decision. She was worried about what will their families think of it. Nevertheless, for Bilal his friends and comrades always had his back. They both got married in a local Gurudwara in Sikh customs.

"Papa?" Bilal came out of his metaphysical realm.it was Hari. The boys are up.
"You are up. Where is Balvi?" Bilal asked
"There he is'. Balvi was looking at the skyscrapers. He was mesmerised by the evening colour show at the sky.

The ship was almost full. MV Kavaritti was about to commence its voyage. Balvi was watching the evening sun. Bilal put his hand through his shoulders. Bilal was often felt that the boys were not able to overcome the loss of their mother. No children will ever easily come across the loss of their mother. Now all he had was these children. A Crippled ex-soldier on a ship to Lakshadweep with twin boys having Punjabi names and a Patka on their head. It was seemed to be a weird combination for some. It might be the same reaction of his mother. But Bilal knows there is always more room in his mother's loving heart. It was a long 8 years. He was not there when his father passed away three years ago. Nor he could be there for Sadiq, his big brother when he passed away recently.

* * *

He bought both the boys towards him. He felt he was not strong as he used to be. That night changed everything. It was freezing on the snowy Pir Panchal. There was some random firing in the evening upon the bunker. However, he never thought of a large-scale shelling on that night. There was an explosion. He was fainted. The next thing he knew was that, he was in a bed in the Military hospital of Jammu. He was tired. He could not remember anything more. Suddenly had a feeling that he was very weak. He realised that he lost his left leg. Harsh was next to his bed. He was awake long before Bilal. Harsh lost his left arm from the shelling.

"Looks like I have to do my entire business with a single hand". He cracked a terrible joke at Bilal.
"You could join some circus" Bilal grinned.

It was bloody combat. Sukdev and Praksah are no more. Bilal was already prepared for something like this a long time ago. Any soldier posted on the front would at least give a thought of being martyred or crippled. After Spending some weeks in the hospital, he was discharged. He was provided with a prosthetic leg, which will perform the functions of his lost leg. First, he struggled with the prosthetic leg. He neither could not walk properly nor could he balance it. Even Harmsirat was worried when he handled the boys. Anyhow, a crippled man is always crippled. He is no good for any hard labour. He went see Prakash's family, not far away from Gurdaspur. He felt sorry for his young wife and old mother. She only gave birth to a newborn two days ago. Fate was cruel. However, he was worried about something else. His wife and the boys. They mean the whole world to him. The day Harsimrat gave birth to those two healthy boys; Bilal could not believe he bought two new lives in this planet. His military discipline could not hide his emotions. He wished to found his world in them. However, the destiny was cruel. Harsimrat asked him to embrace her one last time while she was on that deathbed of a Cancer ward in Ferozepur hospital. Bilal was hoped for a long life with her but the fate had stored something else. He was shattered. There was nothing much he can do, except give her a pleasant farewell. It has been nearly two months since then. He often thinks that he could not bid her a proper farewell. He was not himself.

He was frozen when he immersed her ashes in Ravi.
'What are you thinking?" Bilal asked Balvi.

"About Maa". Balvi said. Bilal could not say anything. He tightened the grip of his hold. Bilal was Silent for the next couple of minutes. The boys are not expected to see their father with one leg after a long time. Bilal stayed in Mamdot for a while. He was now completely shattered. Sukdeep, his father-in-law felt sorry for himself and for Bilal. He lost his daughter young to ill fate. Bilal was silent for long time. The cold wind blown upon the Punjab plains did not had any effect on him.

In one such of cold nights, Bilal saw the open sky. He could see the stars. Suddenly a cold breeze fondled him. He remembered the sea. He remembered home. The Corals and turquoise water. He and Sadiq used to watch Kavara in nights like this. The blue glowing waves was an extraordinary sight to see. He saw his mom. He felt relieved. Each moment when he thought of home, he felt relieved from the haunting memories of the dark past. The coral dreams were a ray of hope among this dark ocean of grief. He wants his boys to have the same dreams. He wanted them to swim along dolphins. They could see Kavara in nights like this. They could swim together. He will teach them Jeseri. His affectionate mother will teach her grandsons how to write Malayalam Alphabets. She would show them the pictures framed in the wall. The history of their family. She will cook delicious Meenkarry for them. They will have Hisham and Rinsi as their best friends. The boys could see Sabeena, their aunt. They will run along the white sandy beaches of Androth. He will take them to fishing and expedition to the uninhabited islands. Harinder and Balvinder will not be some strangers on that island. Bilal wanted to show how he had a wonderful childhood. He wanted them to have them; the unexplored part of their heritage. He would take them often to mainland to explore more. Bilal opened his eyed from the dream. It was as if a divine angel was there to show him the brighter part of the side. Sukdeep does not had any objection. He wanted them to have normal childhood devoid of more pain and grief in their life.

MV Kavaritti was moving away from the dock. The ancient waters of Kochi were bidding farewell. The phantom vessels of the past belonging to the Dutch, Portuguese, Chinese, Roman, Egyptians had entered to the ancient port through this Small opening or Kochu Azhi.

When the dawn break in the east, the ship was near to an island. It was like an emerald in a turquoise water. The Coconut palms trees shaped the skyline of the island. For the boys, it was nothing like they have seen. They are about to visit their own heritage. Bilal Nallakoya was back at home after long eight years. The ship could not near the docks due to heavy wind. Some trolley fishing boats sailed through the turquoise waters to take the passengers from the ship to the island. Hari and Balvi was scared. They feared of being sinking in those waters. However, at the same time the enchanting corals mesmerised them. Bilal set foot on the white sandy beach of Androth. A chapter in his life has ended. He took the children with them along the narrow concrete road and passed an old tiled building made of coral stones. That was the shrine of Sheikh Ubaidulla, a medieval saint venerated across the islands. The entire island seemed to be a new world to the boys. Last time Bilal walked through the sands, he had two legs. Now he had extra four legs. He stopped in front of an old tiled mansion. Nalla Koya Manzil. An old woman was drying Copra in front of the house.

Umma? Bilal called with a weak voice.

Beekunji never expected it. She was unable to say something. It was her only surviving son. She burst in to tears and the next thing she did was hugging and kissing her son as like she has not seen him for a century. She was curious with two kids with a patka on their heads. Hari and Balvi hide behind their father. Beekunji embraced them.

She thanked the almighty for giving back her son with two sweet grandsons.

Time was paused from then.

That night Bilal saw a dream. He was in the snowy mountains. He was with full battle gear with heavy ammunitions. He could barely walk with his prosthetic leg. An intense battle. Sounds of shelling and cries. He saw bloody wounded soldiers. Blood was everywhere. Bunkers were burning. He does not know what to do. He looked surroundings. It was insane. Bilal yelled. Yelled like a lunatic. Then suddenly it all went blank. There was a park. He was sitting next to Harsimrat. His head on her lapse. She was fondling his dark hair. He used love that. Bilal was enjoying it. Suddenly the soft hands turned into some sharp claws. Everything was blank again. He saw a clear sky. Sandy beaches of Androth. The boys are swimming. He and Harsimrat was watching them from the beach.

STORY - IV

LIFE AFTER RETIREMENT

ASHISH KHANDARE

LIFE AFTER RETIREMENT

"How difficult it is for a Soldier to begin the life of a civilian after retirement?" I am an ex-army soldier. I always had an ambition to work for Army from my childhood. I used to imagine an exciting life of a soldier. But when I joined Indian Army, while in training itself, I understood that it's not going to be easy. It requires a huge dedication and lots of sacrifices in life. After all, we put our own life on stake, which is, of course, not easy task. Generally, everybody talks about love and to die for love. We soldiers actually take on death head to head and move ahead with big heart to fight with enemies for safety of our nation. After working so many years in army, I was happy but nervous about life without Army. It had become my life to work in army. But you cannot work for Army throughout your life. I had missed my beautiful years of life in Army. When all others enjoyed their puberty or young age we soldiers do not even see if it is a day or night while keeping surveillance of border area. We keep our all emotions aside and concentrate on our duty for nation. Our duty becomes our first priority. After working with a tough routine like this for so many years, emotion goes away from your heart. You become more rigid & emotionally tough person.

At home, now I was able to give a quality time to my wife, my children and my parents as well. I have missed them for long time. Initially, I thought that everybody had been missing me too. They all would be not only happy but would be overwhelmed by my presence in home for lifetime. Initial few days, were very much exciting and had happy moments at my home each and every day. I enjoyed attention of my wife and children who had now grown up.

But in few days, I had started feeling that I was missing my charm in life. I started feeling that life had become boring at home. As I had spent my major life in studying, training and working, my ways of enjoyment were different than what a normal citizen would have. I was not enjoying chit chatting with friends or family. I was not enjoying watching TV or Movies which my wife and children would do daily. I was getting irritated when; my children would not wake up early in the morning. They had even started telling me that I have become very much boring dad now. My wife and children were always on mobile phones either chit chatting on social media or talking to their friends. It was little tough for me to get active on social media. My friends, who were also soldiers, were facing similar issues.

Initially, I started putting my disciplinary actions on children. But today's children are smart as they do not believe in hard work. Rather they started telling me to change. I had started getting frustration with myself and made me think if I am wrong in trying to put discipline in children.

Now my daily routine was much different than what I had been used to. Day to day activities, like grocery, managing household

* * *

things was taking my full day to understand as I had never done or got involved in these routine works earlier in my life. Nobody had told me to bring vegetables from market. I still remember my first day in market. One man was selling vegetables. First, selection of vegetables is not your decision. You have to select which your children like. Earlier when I used to come home for holidays, my wife used to cook all my favourite curries. But now, before I step out for buying vegetables, my wife gives me long list of instructions about fruits and vegetables I need to bring as they are children's favourite. But that's not at all a concern. I too love and care for children. As a father, I too have to think about my children's likes and dislikes. Problem would start after I reach home with bag full of vegetables and fruits. After going through the tedious job of selecting, picking and paying the bills, when I reach home, my wife would scream at not being careful in picking the good quality of vegetables. Some of the vegetables would already be rotten and some were about to get rotten. And when she heard the amount, I paid for this, she put her hand on her head and said "God only can save you! You wasted money as well as vegetables." I felt so cheated. People have a very short memory and they forget very soon that this person has devoted his best part of his life for their safety.

Now daily when I go to shop, I start fighting with the shop keeper for not giving good vegetables to avoid getting cheated. As a soldier, we get angry for any nonsense activity. I took long time to adjust with this situation. Somehow, I managed to cope up with society now.

Doing business is another story. As I am at home, my parents and wife decided that I should do some business. When I started researching on different types of businesses, I realized that, business is nothing but a factory of lies. And as a soldier, I can't bear lies. I started getting irritated when I see people lie for small reasons to make money. In our army office if any soldier tells lie, he would get punishment. After all, honesty of Army only keeps nation safe and democracy alive. Otherwise, we have seen some countries getting destroyed due to rising of corruption in their military.

I always felt that India should implement the rule of Solider training mandatory for all in schools like some countries are already doing. This will improve discipline and realization of responsibility towards nation in children. My two qualities, Truthfulness and Discipline, which I used to consider as my strengths have now become my weaknesses. My family started getting irritated with me as these qualities would no longer work in the society to get success. They were sure that I would fail in any business if I continue to stick to these qualities.

The most irritating thing in our society is corruption. Corruption is so imbibed in the nerves of most government officials and citizens, that nobody thinks it as a wrong practice. But as an ex-army soldier, I tried to resist the corruption. But I didn't have anyone from my family or the society to support me. My pension was stuck due to the corruption.

Slowly I am learning this new life. I am learning to talk lies. I am learning to adjust with indiscipline. I am learning to unlearn my army training as now I have to live my life as a normal civilian.

STORY - V

THE BATTLE OF A SOLDIER

RAJEEV A. MASIH

THE BATTLE OF A SOLDIER

The protagonist of the story, an ex-army man reaches the Jaipur Junction where he faces an unexpected battle which brings a strong realization in him.

What was the battle faced by the protagonist and who wins at the end or is it a final truce?

For these enthralling questions to be answered, please read the thoughtful fiction –

'The Battle Of A Soldier' by Rajeev A. Masih.

1.   Mr. Surjan Pal Samudra at the Jaipur junction.

It was nearing to eight in the night of the November month, when Mr. Surjan Pal Samudra had reached the Jaipur junction with his luggage, a small polished iron trunk and a shoulder bag. The middle-aged man in the late thirties was dressed in a heavy brown shirt and loose jeans to combat the light chill in that part of the country.

As there was a still a good number of minutes for the Aravali Express, a direct train from Jaipur to Mumbai to arrive for the boarding of the passengers, Mr. Surjan, had occupied a seat on the platform, meant for the passengers and had kept his luggage aside on the floor.

2.   A Soldier's Flashback.

After having surveyed the entire vicinity by his sight, Mr. Surjan had closed his eyes to the present surroundings of the junction and was completely lost in his thoughts - Thoughts which had started with his resident ship in Mumbai in a small flat of 45 sqft with his parents, his selection as a soldier in the Indian army and then being posted at the Rajasthan border.

His occasional visits to his small house, his marriage followed by the birth of a daughter and then the death of his parents, one after another.

Later, he had been diagnosed of a case of chronic jaundice and had moved an application to his superiors for a Pre mature retirement from his duties as a soldier while being in the army.

His application had been accepted on the basis of his affected health condition and he had been relieved from his post at the Rajasthan border.

Presently, the soldier Surjan Pal Samudra was feeling a variety of emotions. He was sad on leaving the army and all his compatriots, combined with the feeling of a joy of being reunited with his family.

3.   A Soldier Versus the Common Lot.

And while he was still roaming in the world of his thoughts, he was rudely jolted somewhat by a woman who was more on the heavier side of the weight; dressed in a traditional saree and a shawl covering her shoulders.

"Move aside, this seat is meant for more than one person.", said the woman in a haughty way.

For a minute, the soldier was filled with anger on seeing the impunity of the woman and wanted to give her a piece of his mind, especially when he was already seated on the corner part of the seat, leaving sufficient space for anyone to sit comfortably.

Still, he quietly, edged himself more on the side of the seat and the woman very gruffly sat down.

Soon after, she took out her mobile phone from her ladies' hand bag and started complaining loudly about her daughter in law, to the other person on the line.

Mr. Surjan was clearly feeling disturbed and began to look around while making sure that the edge of the seat on which he was seated was not trespassed.

4. Interesting Sights.

As the soldier started to glance around, the sights appeared to be quite interesting and sufficient to keep him distracted, compared to the nonsense talk to which he was being forced to listen.

In a short distance to the seat, stood a newlywed couple and their public display of affection was an ample proof of their entry into matrimony.

Next to the couple sat a middle-aged husband and wife, hardly talking to the other, leave apart even their looking at each other. Mr. Surjan, smiled to himself on seeing the two contrasts of a married life and began to see a similarity of his own marital state with the second couple.

5. Love for Political Parties?

A group of three men could be over heard venting their opinions on the political matters of the country and the way they were supporting some or the other political parties, it appeared to be a matter of time only before they would be entering into scuffles with each other in a ratio of 2:1.

A frown erupted on the soldier's face which showed his strong dislike for politics.

He could remember very clearly, the hard life of the Indian soldiers who stay separated from their families for the maximum time of the year, facing the tough conditions and the enemy at the same time.

The uncertainty of being attacked and of being killed anytime, yet very much united with the other soldier brother while here in the safety of their areas, some of these 'civilians' were clearly divided and would squabble and even kill someone over petty political matters.

Their loyalty to their political parties made him wonder, that would they be that much devoted to the motherland too or was it a love only for their political parties and their ideologies?

6. The Arrival Of The Train and An Un-invited Delay.

Mr. Surjan's line of thoughts were disturbed by the arrival of the train which made the waiting passengers run towards the locomotive as if it would depart without boarding of the passengers, and this impatience of the people had only resulted in chaos at the entry gates of the bogies.

The soldier stood at the last of the badly formed line, without uttering a word. His mind raced to the systematic queue formation and the discipline found in the army.

On entering the bogey, the retired soldier searched for his seat and soon found it.

It was a lower berth and he comfortably sat on it after tying his luggage with a chain and keeping the two articles under the seat properly.

Not much time had passed when the other fellow passengers stepped in the bogey and one by one began to occupy their respective seats.

Somewhere at a distance, the horn of the train was heard, indicating its departure and then within five minutes, the train had slowly started chugging on its way.

Everything appeared to be going smoothly but hardly had the train left the station when suddenly it began to slow down and then it stopped with a jerk.

Apparently, someone had pulled the chain which had halted the movement of the train.

Mr. Surjan muttered something inaudible which most probably must have been a curse.

"Surely some idiot must have pulled down the chain." Thought the ex-army man.

A complete twenty minutes later, while everyone was pondering over the sudden stoppage of the train, the reason became clear. It was indeed a notorious act of some highly irresponsible person who's relative had not stepped down when the train had started and so the related passenger had decided to stop the train by pulling down the chain, so as to enable his relative to get down from the train.

The soldier looked at his wrist watch, being fully aware that once a train is stopped by pulling down its chain, the action disrupts the entire time table of the system and thereby a late arrival at the destination is stamped.

7. Comparisons.

A look of irritation flashed on the ex-army soldier's face as he really hated a wastage of time.

"How can a country progress when the citizens are only concerned about their fundamental rights but not their fundamental duties?"

He spoke aloud for the first time as the other passengers too expressed their anger on the stoppage of the train.

The zeal of a soldier living within Mr. Surjan, began to compare the systematic way of the army to the erratic behaviour of some of the civilians.

How much preferable was the life of a soldier in the defence services was evident by the way, Mr. Surjan Pal Samudra fondly recalled his number of years in the army.

8. No Hate Towards Anyone.

It was not that he hated the common people, the civilians. No, he had nothing against anyone in general or in particular but it was the carelessness, the 'for granted' attitude of his countrymen which at times got on his nerves, such that it troubled him only. He very much realized that one's entry in the army brings a momentous change in the personality of a person and it is all because of a zeal, a passion and an excitement of serving one's country and of being prepared to die for the nation.

Mr. Surjan Pal Samudra, stared up at the point, where the chain to stop the train was installed and an instant thought flashed over his mind.

"The liberty to pull a chain to stop a train, the freedom to show public display of affection, the emancipation to squabble over political matters and the liberation to complain of one's daughter in law; all, yes, all of it exists only because the borders of a country are protected by the sacrifices of the soldiers."

With this thought, the soldier, Surjan Pal Samudra, relaxed and smiled, the train had still not started.

It was for sure, that there will be a delay of few hours before he will be able to reach to his house, in Mumbai – 'Welcome to the world of the civilians.'

STORY - VI

THE TRAIL OF LIFE

DEESHA SONI

THE TRAIL OF LIFE

Zoraver Singh was on a regular morning jog at the nearest jogger's park... it's been his routine ritual since he had retired after his services from the Indian Army...

Though Zoraver Singh had got mature looks with his ripening age...he still was robust in stature standing 6.2 ft tall with a handlebar moustache... partially bald head... a stalwart voice... were his personality traits...

Zoraver Singh... lived like an army man most of his life.... a true disciplinarian... After a month of his retirement...he still was stuck to his schedule of morning jogs at the neighbourhood jogger's track...

While alike the army culture Zoraver Singh was an early riser.... while his homemates were up quite late.... this fact pricked Zoraver Singh like a thorn ....as he expected his homemates to follow discipline....

Zoraver Singh sat at a bench nearby with sadness on his face and thoughts hovering his mind.... as Initially Zoraver Singh was happy about the fact that he is back among his people at home... proudly serving the Indian Army... but as days passed Zoraver

Singh realised that there was a constant friction between his familymates and him in thoughts and action...

This friction of views and lifestyle then turned into a bitter truth eventually... between Zoraver Singh and his familymates... each time Zoraver Singh tried to bring a set of rules and code of conduct... it was rudely brushed aside by his grown-up children...as they wanted their own freedom and set rules....

Even Zoraver Singh's wife .... was not in terms with Zoravers ideologies.... she had no issues if their children came late from parties or didn't perform morning prayers...or weren't physically active....

Zoraver Singh's family mates made insulting remarks....and questioned Zoraver Singh's presence for his wife and children for many years when they needed Zoraver Singh emotionally and physically in their growing up years...and his dedication solely for his nation and ignorance towards family....

Zoraver Singh still was sitting on the bench...in the mid of his jogging...and tearful silence and deep thoughts of the behavior of his familymates towards him... harsh and neglectful....

Zoraver Singh suddenly got up from the bench at the joggers track as if he had made up his mind.... for something concrete...and thick....

● ● ●

Zoraver Singh boarded a train to Himachal Pradesh.... from his city of residence Delhi and started a new goal far away from judgemental and eyebrow raising people.... Zoraver Singh shortly joined as a trainer at the Army public boarding school amid scenery and natural peace and beauty.... here Zoraver Singh's teachings were followed, observed and respected by the youth students of the school.... Zoraver Singh's stories which he narrated to the students were awed and applauded... with whistles and claps....

Years passed at the Army public boarding school.... though repeated attempts from his familymates to bring him back failed until they finally gave up on their pleadings of calling Zoraver back home....

One day the old Zoraver Singh was sitting at his cozy room by the fire lit writing his story.... named 'The trail of life'....and smog of the winters covered the entire surroundings.... Zoraver Singh's pen suddenly slipped off from his hand...and his head rested on the book of his writings... Zoraver Singh was numb, pale and cold.... his trail of life had stopped...

His students and the staff rushed by him....in panic... only to find Zoraver Singh dead in silence.... life had departed... flapping it's wings....

Later.... Zoraver Singh's book 'The trail of life' came in print.... after his demise.... which turned out to be one of the most read book of the year.... Yet...the man Zoraver Singh who gave up most part of his life for his country.... faced negligence and cold ignorance from his family mates... to be recognized by others....and praised by the distant ones.... who knew the worth of Zoraver Singh...and his Trail of life'......

⸺◦◇◦⸺

STORY - VII

PIECES OF ROSE

RABI CHATTERJEE

PIECES OF ROSE

1st Scene

There was a firing going on. Some soldiers had already died. Blood, chunks of their bodies were spattered around everywhere. Prashant took shelter behind a tree. The place was a little away from their room. Just an hour back some terrorists had attacked their troops and it caught them unaware. It happened suddenly. Firing has been going on since dawn. All those terrorists were lying died. Some soldiers were groaning. They were fighting with their life. There was no hospital nearby. So, they were treating themselves. After a long and bloodshed days of shooting, few alive soldiers took shelter in a jungle. Now the situation was under their control. The firing had stopped, though they were not 100% sure about the count of the attackers. It was very much possible that some of the terrorists would have taken shelter nearby and they could begin firing again. The morning passed and it was afternoon. The jungle was calm. Those alive soldiers were taking rest but cautiously.

Again, another round of firing.

2nd Scene

Prashant woke up suddenly on his bed. He turned his backs against the bed. Beside him, his wife was sleeping. A dim light was gleaming in their room. It was 4 in the morning. He got up from the bed and went to the washroom. Then came back to his room and checked if their 8-year-old son, Snehil was sleeping soundly in the next room. Snehil usually used to sleep with his mother when his father was away serving. As his father was home, he was sleeping in his own room. He picked the towel from the hanger. There was a mirror behind the towel. He saw himself in the mirror. His army suit was hanging beside it. He took a glance at it. His name was still glowing on the badge. Then he saw the mirror. He had put on some weight.

Some questions were reflecting in his mind.
Who is this? Is this the old soldier?

He went to his bed, checked his wife, kissed her forehead and slowly kept his head on the bolster.

Prashant retired from the army last year. Now, he was settled with his family. But something was disturbing him. He could understand that it was loneliness, depression, frustration because he didn't have anything to do except bringing his son from the school, talking to friends over the phone and spending time with family and taking them outside sometimes. There was no known friend who he would spend time with him. Their apartment was in a good society. He used to spend his time with neighbours but deep inside him, he knew he was missing the old days, old friends in the army. He missed the regular hard-core training, their friendship, and sharing knowledge about different culture. Now he was feeling total empty. Recently, his drinking habit had also increased. To appease the mental disorientation, drinking was the only option for him. He could keep his mind calm for a few hours. His wife could understand the problem. She told him to learn something or do some other jobs to keep himself busy. But he couldn't yet decide what he would do.

3rd *Scene*

Prashant was lying on his bed and looking at the ceiling fan. He was staring at it so meditatively. Fan was running and Prashant was absorbed by its rhythm. His wife called him from kitchen asking what time it was. He couldn't even hear her. She came and turned off the fan. His attachment with the rhythm also broke.

"What are you doing? How long will you be like this?", Sumedha asked.
"Oh sorry, what happened?"
She took the bread out of the refrigerator and went to the kitchen. He followed her.
Sorry Sumedha, he apologized.
I told you to do something, Sumedha said. Please don't stay like this. Otherwise, you will get mad one day.
Yes, of course, I'll do, he said.
But when? She asked.
There was a long silence.

"Okay, it's almost 1pm. Its time to pick Snehil from the school. Please go and bring him home", Sumedha said.

● ● ●

He checked the clock on the wall. It was 1:10. The time for their son's return from school.

"Okay", he said, while putting on his shirts. He steps out from home.

4th Scene

Inside the bathroom, Prashant started crying with frustration without making any noise. He couldn't get accustom to the current situation. Post-traumatic syndrome had acquired him. He used to keep a diary when he was in the battalion but now, it was his seldom companion. Only alcohol could appease his mental disorder. Earlier while still serving rarely he would drink. He would often tell his friends that drinking alcohol reduces the thinking power which is not good for us in Army. But now he started drinking regularly at night after his son slept.

This night too, Prashant is sitting and drinking.

Sumedha asked, "What's wrong with you, Prashant?"

"What happened now?" he countered.

"Why aren't you doing some constructive work? May be start a business or take up part time consulting work? Do you realize the harm you are doing to your mental and physical health by simply sitting idle and drinking?"

"I told you many times, Sumedha, of course, I will do," he replied. "Give me some time."

The chaos was graining in their relationship. They started to fight on every little thing. Sometimes, they would go to bed starving because they would fight and none of them will have dinner.

Snehil was also getting disturbed at what was happening in his family.

"Ma is coming tomorrow", Sumedha said.

"When?"

"Tomorrow morning"

"Any one coming with her?"

"Yes, your brother-in-law"

"Hmmm"

5th Scene

The next day, her mother came with her little brother to visit them. Sumedha shared all the trouble she was facing in their relationship with her mother. Her brother, Subhash was talking to Prashant.

How long will you stay like this? Subhash asked. You also realize that what is going between you and my sister.

Yes, I know, Prashant replied.

Tell me if I can help you with anything, Subhash said.

Sure, Prashant said.

Please, don't let the strife affect Snehil, Subhash concluded.

He was silent with them most of the time because he knew what was going on with him.

6th Scene

Prashant started to share his writing on a Facebook group. After gaining some appreciation on social media, he started writing again. Every day whatever came in his mind, he would captivate in his diary. Now again his love for diary writing started growing. He started writing more and more. He started feeling better and now he was lot less stressed. His following on Facebook also increased and people would appreciate his writing. His followers crossed 10 Lakhs and had over 1000 posts in a span of just 9 months. He took creative writing classes online, to hone the skills. There was happiness inside him. He found a new attraction in writing. His mental state started to improve gradually. Short stories, poetries, daily feelings were his regular jobs. He felt a little refreshed again.

7th Scene

"Hello, is this Book Pride literary publication?", He asked over the phone.

"Yes, tell me, how may I help you?" the answer was from the opposite side.

"Would you kindly check if my work suits to be published?" he asked.

The voice on the other side asked Prashant to send them 4 chapters from the manuscript through e-mail and wait for their response. When Prashant asked how soon he can expect a reply, the person on the phone told his that the whole process can take 4-6 months.

Prashant ended the conversation by thanking him for the information.

He wrote many things in a few months. Now, he wanted to publish his work. He was looking for some magazines, publishing houses who would print his work. He called many publishing houses but everyone asked him to send the sample manuscript and asked him to wait for months.

Again, Prashant was feeling dejected and sad. But things changed one day.
Prashant receives a call on his cell phone.
"Hello, is this Prashant?"
"Yes."

"We loved your creative work 'Pieces of rose' and we are interested to publish it. Can we discuss it further?"
Prashant's happiness knew no bounds.
Prashant succeeded in publishing his book. Now he is an established author. He is living happily with his family.

STORY - VIII

HE IS A SOLDIER

SAHELI BANERJI

HE IS A SOLDIER

My father was in the army. For twenty-five years, he served our country, sacrificing everything that he held within. He was the son of a zamindar family, the landed aristocrats of Palasdanga. My great grandfather was given the title of Bahadur for his fierce indomitable spirit. My father is the only son of my grandpa and naturally, he inherited everything. The landed substantial mansion, the lands, the orchards, the ponds and so much more. He could have settled in our ancestral village and ruled like a benevolent king. Or he could have sold everything and settled with us in some satellite city. He did neither. From early childhood, he was distinct. When his friends aimed to secure a government job and lead a luxurious life, he sat on NDA and CSB exams.

The life of a soldier always enticed him. The zeal to serve the motherland, the pride to stand upright on the border and guarding the country, the glory to become a martyr in the battle attracted him as a flame does to a moth. It was from his reason he ran off from home when the appointment letter from IMA arrived. He knew my grandmother would never allow her only son to join the army and die in foreign lands far away from the blood kins. So he got away. Ran away in the dead of a night, boarded the train to Jabalpur, and straight to the Indian army

Centre for training Institute. What happened when he returned home after a year of training shunning his curly hair for a crew cut hairstyle is a story for another day!

Those twenty-five years were the best time of his life. Other than meeting with my mother and marrying her, he had his full share of happiness in his work too. Training personnel, mock war practices, gunfights, horse riding, and evening with his chummy! Those were the days! He often narrated to us about his life on Border.

"It is the most beautiful place anyone can ever reach to see. White snow-capped mountains everywhere your eyes fall upon, clear blue sky, and a temperature is less than minus 20 degrees. It's a glory to stand there with the flag fluttering high as if they say 'you are not alone. I am with you' the whole country sleeps while we stand awake and alert, guarding our motherland with our lives".

I still remember that time when the Kargil war broke out between India and Pakistan. My father was posted at Rajouri Border for six months. That was the time when the internet was still a baby inside the womb of a computer that was still a child itself. Everything was curtailed, with no rights no liberties no freedom. Even letters used to be used long after the writer has already deceased. Such was the situation! Every day scores of soldiers perished. The Delhi Doordarshan flooded its channel with the news of war, the martyrs, and the fake consolatory speeches of different ministers of government. We didn't care for those. We didn't care who was in power or who held the sceptre. For us, only the life of one man mattered. We used to wait with paved breath for just one single news.

Those six months made me realize that life is no better than the holocaust for a family whose father, husband, and son go to war. Those six months were a trial for us too. It was as if we were fumbling for each other in the dark. My mother tried her best to remain strong but I knew about her silent sobbing in the kitchen at night. I was too young to understand the real implication of war then, but now I can very well comprehend how each of us went through the harrowing hell in that long span of six months. The only human who suffered the most was my grandmother. She almost left her eating and sleeping. Day after day, night after night she spent counting the beads of her rosary and praying for the safety of my father. Probably the gods heard her prayer and he returned hale and hearty after six months.

When he returned home, we came to see how brutal a war came to be. A young soldier who was napping just two meters away from my father after a frozen meal of stale chapatti and pickle was shot dead by a flying bullet. He never got up to see the rising sun the next morning. There was a bomb blast a foot apart from their embankment. Stories like this filled my heart with bitterness. What was the use of the war? Nothing did change. We are still fighting uselessly.

The old lie: Dulce et decorum est
Pro Patria Mori

Our lives rotated around these stories, waiting for his arrival after every six months on station to see the middle-aged crew cut tall man step out from the compartment and swept both of us into his arms. that was our lives. Fear of losing him made us stronger. But the strongest was my mother. Never once she broke down crying when left every time, never once she tried to stop him. She said to me once," your father's dedication towards his nation made me fall in love with him. Everyone should do his part in serving the country however little it might be".

I can never be like mom. Although I have inherited my father's indomitable spirit and urge to explore the world, I can never be a strong-hearted woman like my mom. I am more like my grandma, emotional, compassionate, and weak.

Then that day came when it was time for him to step down, put his uniform away into the closet, and his tired old body to rest. He retired after serving his motherland for two decades and more. The hardest days were yet to come. We always were habituated to seeing him in his military routine. Post-retirement hit him hard. There was no mission, there was no target, there was no goal. He felt himself stumbling in darkness, with nothing to do, nothing to achieve, and a complete aimless human. My mother started giving him some household chores to do like buying vegetables, cleaning the car and the bike, brushing the dust off the couches, and so on. Those things were new for him. Before he joined the army, my father was a precious darling of grandma. He passed his time with football and music swinging his curly hair and making the ladies of those eras sigh in love!

Things changed when he joined the military. He became a hard-hearted man, crew-cut hair, well-built muscular who carried his AK 47 all along. A man like that didn't look good buying potatoes and dusting dirt every day. The more he tried to saturate himself in that life, the more he lost his mental peace.

Every soldier passes this phase of his life. As long as he serves the nation, he is remembered. No sooner he turns into an aged horse, he is turned out. No one remembers him, no one congratulates him, and no one gives him a road and a salute for his long service. Frustration creeps in slowly. My father too was not accustomed to that pathetic life. As days passed, he became more irritated. My mother advised him to start working somewhere. That would keep his mind distracted. Indian government gives a quota for military ex-servicemen to start work after their retirement into other semi-governmental agencies as security officers and other posts. But was it easy for a middle-aged man to carry his CV and high resumes and attend interviews and seminars for a job? No, it wasn't.

By god's grace we had enough to provide for our means, so earning money to support a family wasn't necessary for my father. He passed his time, looking at his medals caressing them. I realized this is what the life of every soldier turns into once he gets retired from the battlefield. Depressed. Dilapidated and alone. Although he was present with us physically, his mind was far away.

When a child is upset, parents are bound to intervene in his personal life. So is with the gods. There came a time when the Gods probably decided to intervene in our lives personally and solve the matter that we were going through. They sent a reward for his service.

Brijbasi Mahamant came to our home. Tall well built in an orange attire with wooden sandals and a beaded rosary in one hand and a bundle in his shoulder, he spread an aura of serenity in our lives. He came of his own accord. No one knew why or what his intention was. But we were never inquisitive towards those things. His smiling face and his ways of explaining the Bhagwad Gita mesmerized us. We felt our souls rejuvenated, our thirst for knowledge mitigated, and our desire to know the unknown was satisfied. His voice was deep and sonorous, like the deep bells of an ancient temple, whose sound vibrates through all the walls of the God's abode. He was the harbinger of peace for my father. My father was never a God-fearing man. He was a theist but the relationship between him and Almighty was just as formal as two neighbours crossing paths. But that day everything changed. The way he revealed to him the secrets of life, the true meaning of his truer self, the path of salvation, and the logic behind the trans-migration of soul, brought tears into my father's eyes. Never had we seen a man with such high impulse like an ADHD patient, sit still like a rock, trying to restrain his emotional overflow.

"Who is a soldier?", asked Brijbasi
-"One who fights for his motherland", replied my father.

-"Really? Just only for the motherland? What about the one who fights for evil?"

My father was speechless. This never had crossed his mind.
-"Do you know who is a True Soldier? Son, a true soldier is who fights with evil. one who guards his fellow beings against evil, from darkness, from satan. One who protects his loved ones from evil."

-"What is evil?"
-"It's not an enemy state or a nation. It's not a physical entity. It's not a terrorist. It's us. Simply us"
-"us? How?"

Brijbasi smiled. A sparkle crinkled in the corner of his eyes.
"Evil resides within us. Deep inside our soul. That's what prevents us from Moksha. That's what stops us from leaving the cycle of birth and death. It's evil inside men which cause war, it's evil inside men which wages battles and which creates a lust for more".

My father was astounded. He simply looked at him wide-eyed, in amazement.
"son, can you fight with that?"
-"can I?"

-"yes. You can. You are a soldier. Once a soldier will always be a soldier. You are born for this. You have crossed levels and pathways and cross yards in this game of war. Now you are in here. In this level to fight another battle. You have already fulfilled your duty as a son of this pious land. Now fulfil your duty as a destroyer of evil in mankind".

-"But how?"
He touched my father's hand and patted him.

"look around you. The world is dying. Each day thousands of men, women, and children are perishing in vices and follies of their own. Think of a single man whom you can save from being corrupted. Think of a single soul you can protect from succumbing to the dark. Even you can save one man, one soul and one living thing, your battle as a soldier will not go waste".

Realization dawned upon us. He felt as if a window has been opened in the darkroom that pervaded upon him all this time. His soul relaxed, his contorted face smoothened and his lost smile returned. His eyes sparkled again and he felt a strong adrenaline rush that once flowed into his veins.

Brijbasi got up and blessed us with wide open hands. On the door, He turned around and looked directly at my father and said:

"On the fields of Kurukshetra millions perished. The fight was between good and evil. But which of the soldiers do you still remember? "

STORY - IX

HOMECOMING

DR. SURYA KALADHAR

HOMECOMING

Arvind went to the railway station, to pick up some exciting things that his parents sent from Guntur, his native, to Hyderabad. They had sent a lot of his favourite eatables and pickles – blended in with mother's love, village styled dresses, and toys for his children. When he approached the station, found that the train was early. He ran onto the platform to collect the things from – a person who was so pale, he could have been a ghost. He took the package in haste, but while on the walk back to his car, his mind went back to the person who handed him all the goodies. A middle-aged person with a very familiar voice, initially Arvind could not place the man. And then his mind raced back to some 30 years earlier, when the two men were co-workers in a factory. Due to some difference of opinion, they had stopped meeting each other.

Instead of sitting in the car driving home, Arvind found himself sitting under a neem tree lost in his thoughts, reflecting on his current problems – and they were numerous. As he was replaying the days of past in his mind, he looked up, the ghostly man was standing right in front of him. The seemingly sudden appearance of this man, shocked him, a shiver ran up his spine – he was fear struck.

"Don't be scared! I have come to help you."

"What do you want?"

"I just told you. To help you."

"What? Why? I mean why do you think I need help?"

The Ghost smiled knowingly.

"Why would you want to help me? What is in it for you." Arvind waited for a reply. Still no answer. He continued, "How can you help me?" A pause and then, "What do you want from me?"

At this the man, no the ghost, the ghostly man replied, "You have to wear my face for three days. Never reveal the truth to anyone. Or else the power will be lost."

"Oh! You really are a... a... a... ghost?" Arvind could not find a better word to describe what he thought the entity before him was. But as soon as he blurted the question, he was embarrassed. He had never before believed in super-natural beings. But somehow in his heart he knew he was right. This was not a normal man. It was not a man. Just a mere reflection of what men look like. It was a ghost.

"What is the power," asked Arvind?

The ghost didn't seem to want to answer any of Arvind's queries. He wasn't a talker. In no way did he try to persuade Arvind. Yet there was no need for any convincing. Everything the ghost said, felt true in Arvind's heart. And yet the uneasiness, years of survival skills were sending him warning signals. Only if they

* * *

could be clear on the message – what was it about this ghost that left him apprehensive. But at this point his curiosity was stronger than his fear.

"After three days I will come back. And if you passed the test – wearing my face and not telling anyone about our deal – I will relieve you of my face and give you a diamond globule. As long as the diamond stays on you, you will get all that your heart desires. But remember, you have to keep it on your person all the time. And you will have anything in the world."

Arvind had been facing financial problems. It felt like a God-sent solution. It had to be. The deal looked pretty good. It was simple. Easily do-able. There was nothing to mull over. Arvind immediately agreed.

He went home with the ghostly face. His wife and children could not understand what had happened, and understandably were scared and confused. Arvind did not make things easier for them. Instead of answering their questions, he locked himself in a room. He came out only for food, and that too only when no one was around. He sneaked his meals to the room and bolted it from within. Not knowing what to do, but visibly shaken by what she had briefly seen when Arvind dashed back and forth between his sanctuary of a room to the kitchen, she decided to take advice from the one man they all had always been able to count upon – her father-in-law.

Anusha called Satyamurthy and told him about Arvind's current state. She was out of her wits as to what to do. How could she? She did not even know what was going on. To say Satyamurthy was shocked, would be an understatement. He boarded a train and reached Hyderabad by the next day morning. He tried to ambush Arvind, in hopes of questioning him on what was going on. It was not his character to judge people without giving them a chance to explain themselves first. So he patiently waited till Arvind was ready to put his uneasiness to rest, without coaxing him to explain.

Arvind's father was a big proponent of letting people live their lives. So, he never questioned people's motives, never tried to use his influence to dissuade them from their desires. He would never force his ideals onto his son. But whenever requested he provided Arvind the benefit of his experiences. At this point his son had not solicited his advice, so all he could was ask questions and wait for the replies to come in due time.

Three days passed, with everyone anxious and Arvind wondering if the ghost would keep his word. Arvind arrived at the neem tree - the same place he had talked and accepted the deal with the ghost. That's a weird sentence 'deal with the ghost', and he wondered why the phrase formed in his head. Before he could assess the gravity of the thought he just had had, the ghost did appear. And as was fair, he took back the ghostly parlance and gave Arvind the diamond crystal.

Arvind went back home. Pleased with himself. He had taken a risk; a major risk and he was handsomely rewarded. As he entered the house and saw his father sitting on the sofa reading his newspaper, foreboding and doubts crossed in his mind. But for this once, his risk-taking appetite had beaten his father's teaching of moderation. He had taken a huge risk, trusting something un-worldly. And now was the time to reap hefty dividends. He walked in, grinning ear to ear, and revealed all that had had happened. When he showed them the crystal, his wife and children were overjoyed. They had worked hard all their lives and there was nothing much to show for it. But now, at last they could lead a luxurious life. God knows they deserved it. They had seen lesser talented people have more comfortable lives than theirs. Not anymore. They were getting what was their due. They deserved happiness and now they will have it all.

But his father was not happy at all. He advised Arvind not to rely on such magical things, 'one has to earn honestly to lead a happy life', he cautioned. No one took much notice of his words. Satyamurthy refused to stay with luxuries obtained from invoking the diamond ball, and warned Arvind that his obsession with being rich without work for it will be his downfall. But the family was way too happy to let the warnings of an old man affect their mood.

Satyamurthy had done all that he could do – guide his son and hope his teachings will finally prevail. The honest old man went back to his village. He worked hard, taking care of the little land he possessed. He hired a few helpers and together these farmers grew and some vegetables and were happy with the money they got from selling them. The people working for him were very happy, since they were treated them with respect and dignity as one would their own family. There were compensated well for their work. All in all, Satyamurthy was surrounded by contend hard working people, making a living out of the land of their forefathers – as non-magical and ordinary life that is always skipped over in stories.

* * *

On the other hand, Arvind and his family were living the vision of every dreamer in the world. They now had a big house, multiple cars and all kinds of comforts imaginable.

He did not forget his duties as a son, kept requesting his father to come and stay with him. But the oldman would not oblige.

A tragedy struck at the farm. One of the worker's son met with an accident, and lost both his legs, Satyamurthy stood by him. Since the parents were illiterate, he took care of the educational need of the child and instilled in him the importance of education. The boy was clever, topped his school each year. The teachers and friends were very helpful, so he could continue his studies effortlessly. Arvind's father was very sympathetic towards this boy – Aneesh. After school the Oldman would push little Aneesh in his wheel chair around in the fields. These were the rare moments when Aneesh could be himself – a naughty and playful child. He would pluck fruits and flowers, and play the whole time. Arvind's father and mother enjoyed the little boy's naughty ways and pampered him even more. Aneesh was happy and grateful to the old couple for taking care of him so much. People in the village were curious to see the boy-without-legs study and be happy, as if the handicap had no effect on him. Aneesh was not unaware of what people thought of him of his handicap, but he would not let himself be bogged down by such sympathizers.

Aneesh led a normal life, as everyone at home and school treated him like a normal kid. Aneesh was inspired by his teachers and friends, and felt like a hero. He topped tenth class state board, bringing fame not just to himself but also to the school. Proud of his achievements Arvind's father and mother encouraged him to go for higher studies, joined him in a coaching centre a little further from the village. They sent him by car with a wheel chair and an assistant. A small fortune for their simple means, but they were happy to do so.

Aneesh worked hard securing state third in intermediate and 50th rank in national engineering entrance examination. Got admission into one of the best engineering colleges. With his hard work and good nature, he attracted the attention of teachers and garnered respect of his peers. He was likeable and people around him were always ready to help. Other than studies he would always participate in extra-curricular, obtaining awards in chess and debate. His energy and enthusiasm always inspired around him. Impressed by the boy's personality, and sympathetic of his family background, the faculty gifted him an electrical wheel chair. The gesture gave Aneesh more confidence and made his dream stronger. He got good grades in engineering and got selected in campus selections, got a good job.

* * *

Satyamurthy loved both his sons – the son by birth, who lived in the city in luxury, as well as the boy without legs – son by action – progressing well in his life.

His son in the city was in deep trouble. One day when he took the diamond ball out to make a wish, it slipped out of his hand, rolled on the floor hit the dining table which made the big crystal flower vase turn over and fall down right on the diamond – crushing the tiny ball under its weight. It was difficult to differentiate between the vase shards and diamond bits. Arvind swept all the pieces and gathered them in a box. But the magic was gone. He lost all his wealth, even his house. He had to go the village to his father. When Arvind arrived, ashamed and fatigued, father didn't ask any questions. Asked him to come inside and freshen up. Breakfast was served as if no time had passed, as if the last few years did not happen. After food, the father and son duo were sitting on the verandah, looking at people walking towards the field. Son wanting to say so much but unable to. Father looking ahead in the distance expressionless. Without turning his head towards Arvind, Satyamurthy said, "Don't worry my dear son, we learn a lot from our mistakes. This is just one such lesson. Please relax for a few days. Arvind took a deep breath and felt all his tension dissipating at his father's words.

Then the father told him about the boy with no legs and how he was now settled in life, the boy he treated as his own and came to love as a son. God was merciful at the old man, when one son left another appeared immediately.

Days after his arrival into the village, the prodigal son, started walking to the fields with his father. He didn't realise and he got engrossed in taking care of the fields. His wife started helping the mother-in-law in household responsibilities. The shame the couple felt when they had walked into the house had dissipated. They started taking over the old couple without realising. All things forgotten, the son stayed with father happily, and was proud to have such a father, who had not spoken about his weaknesses, and instead said let's learn from our mistakes.

—●O◇O●—

STORY - X

MISFIT

ANIL KUMAR JASWAL

MISFIT

One day Sooraj was sitting with his beloved in his house in a Malabar village. Both were in romantic mood. And remembering the time when he was in Airforce and he had only annual leave of two months to fulfil all the obligations he had. At that time, he found it very difficult to keep all his family commitments. His wife would always complain that he is in love with the Airforce and not with her. Sometimes, when on exercise he won't be able to give even call to her. And both will miss one another as fish out of water. But he will always convince her with his time-tested excuse i.e., Nation is more important than anything else. And at the same time, he would tell her, "let me come home on leave than I will fulfil all your dreams". But she knew it inside her heart that Sooraj is just respecting her emotions and she respected him for that.

But now he was retired and sitting just at breathes distance from her. As both were deeply involved with one another suddenly rain started falling like hammer and tongs. But as love is blind. They both were not aware what's going on. Everyone in the village is bothered about his Kith and kin. Because village had a small tributary of a river Swan. In rainy season generally it used to overflow and enter in surrounding areas. So, everyone was trying to secure his place. Suddenly somebody said let's take

Sooraj bhai's help for making embankments of the river stronger so that it can't engulf the areas around.

Villagers came to his home and shouted his name time and again but couldn't find a response from a Romeo. Because he was with his Juliet. Then they decided to knock at the door. But again, no avail. Then one youngster applied his mind and went for a video call. As the bell of the mobile phone rang, Sooraj just ignored because he doesn't want to miss the rain and the company of his sweetheart. The youngster tried calling again. His wife asked him to attend the call. She said, there could be something urgent. But again, Sooraj was adamant. He knew his villagers; they will spoil his most beautiful time.

But when third time call came in, his wife was adamant that he takes the call. Seeing her disappointment, Sooraj takes the call. The youngster tells Sooray that whole village is in trouble. The water in the tributary has come up to dangerous level. Sooraj immediately opens the door and goes straight to meet his village people. He leads the villagers and goes to the river bank to handle the upcoming disaster. He immediately knew it was going to be a herculean task for him and his friends as it was raining heavily and very little time they had in their hand.

Sooraj, first searched on Google the NDRF number and dials in from the mobile phone. He also tells the villagers to get some tools. No one at the other end of the phone picks his call. He calls twice and thrice but no response. He really gets jittery. Because of his background of Airforce where he had learnt to respond quickly to any emergencies, he failed to understand why no one in the NDRF is taking up his phone and why any help from the local government administration hasn't come in yet even when villagers had called the local district officers.

Sooray remembers his serving days. If he or his team had not responded to an emergency, they would have to face no less than court marshal and even made them leave the force. Recovering from the shock, he decided to take the matter in his own hands and save the village from the flood. He instructs some of the people to collect the mud, rocks and everything possible to put at the bank so that the flow of water could be stopped.

Sooraj was still trying to get help and he was in no mood to give up. He, then, applies his mind and tries to contact local air commodore of the area. Fortunately, his secretary picks up the call. Sooraj gives his reference and tells him how deeply he and his village is in trouble.

The PS assures him not to worry and promises his that he will get the people of civil works department of Airforce reach to his area and help them to avert the emergency. The secretary asks him if he has retired recently, and tells Sooraj that it will take a while to come to terms with civilian life.

Within an hour, there are people from civil work department comes and takes over the situation and starts working to avoid overflowing of Swan tributary. To Sooraj surprise local MLA rings him and apologies first and promises to send more help. The village was saved. Sooraj learnt how things work in civilian life.

95

PROFILES

AUTHORS
EDITOR
DESIGNER
PUBLISHER

AUTHORS

Anil Kumar Jaswal - Misfit

Anil Jaswal is a part time writer, his work frequently gets published in newspapers, magazines, social media platforms etc. He is a distinguish author of one of the portals. His book titled "Inderdhanush", a collection of 50 poems in Hindi, is published by Notion Press. He has won various awards for his writing.

Ashish Khandare - Life After Retirement

Ashish Ashok Khandare, is an engineer by profession having worked in manufacturing industries like Diebold Nixdorf, Motherson Sumi, Asahi India for more than 16 years. With his professional & personal experiences, he started writing blog on real life short stories and Fictional stories. He has great admiration for Sudha Murthy, Chairperson Infosys Foundation. It is because of her inspiration, he started using simple language so his writing can reach to a bigger audience. He is a very emotional person which reflects in his writing. He is currently writing a book on a story from lockdown India which will be an emotional roller coaster ride. You can check his blogs @ http://beyondthetalebyaj.blogspot.com

Deesha Soni - The Trail of Life

Deesha Soni is a Post Graduate and M. Phil, she adorns the hat of a multitasker as an educationist, artist, poet, photographer, author, homemaker, wife and mother. Writing has come naturally in her genes. She loves trying hands on various genres of literature for Deesha writing is like a therapy which unwinds her thought process and from the mind workshop.

Deesha has various published works to her credit. She has two books published on Amazon, named 'Just thoughts' and 'Random thoughts on pandemic', Kindle edition and more than 100 plus published works on various online platforms of literature. Deesha has been twice nominated for Author of a week award by StoryMirror and has also won various recognitions in penning stories and write-ups both at National and International levels. Deesha is currently penning down yet another work of literature with Amazon Kindle. Her journey has started and has a long way to go along on the path of literature.

Rajeev A. Masih - The Battle of a Soldier

Rajeev A. Masih is passionate about writing. Rajeev started writing fiction and non-fiction work from a very young age of his academic years, he has penned down a plethora of articles, reports, stories, poems and has also delved in the field of blog writing.

He is a double post graduate degree holder in English and in sociology and a professional mentor for almost 19 years. Winner of the third and the fourth prize consecutive time in an online story contest conducted in the year 2020, in the category of the short stories.

Kaweri Mishra - True Calling

Kaweri Mishra is an ex IT professional turned freelance writer from Bangalore. She is a mother and yoga enthusiast. She had a flair for writing since school days. She has written several articles for online media and business content for websites for IT companies. During her stint in IT industry (Infosys ltd), she was involved in writing process and technical documents.

Mridul C Mrinal - Coral Dreams

Mridul C Mrinal is a Poet, Writer and Researcher. His works are mainly in English and Malayalam, he also writes in Hindi, Urdu, Kannada and Tulu languages. Mrinal has been working in various literary fields simultaneously as a Translator and an Author. His works mainly depicts the life of marginalised and disabled sections of the society. A Polyglot himself, Mrinal believes that cultural integrations of various ethno linguistic communities within India and abroad could contribute to the better understanding of the world. He has done his Post Graduate degree in English and Comparative Literature. Mrinal has keen research attitude & presented 12 research papers in various National and International conferences across India. His first work A Malayali gay's Identity: A Study of Kishor Kumar's Randu Prushnmar Chumbikumbol was published in the Anthology Women and Queers: The Marginalized Gender. He worked as an Editorial Assistant to Dr. Efthikar Ahmed on the Anthology of Short stories in Malayalam Titled Akasham Mathram Kanunna Veedukal. His works are published in different Journals of National Importance.

Rabi Chatterjee - Pieces of Rose

Rabi Chatterjee, is a video editor and content writer, he live in Howrah. He is very enthusiastic and self-motivated creative artist who always strives for excellence in his work. Currently, he is freelancing and continuing his graduation in English literature. He is very passionate about - Films, books and internet.

Hari Arayammakul - Monsoon Mischief

Hari Arayammakul is a soldier–turned-writer. Hailing from Kozhikode, Kerala he has travelled extensively across India during his military days. He writes short stories and poems in English and Malayalam. His 'military memoirs' regularly appear in prominent Newspapers like The Hindu, The Deccan Herald and The New Indian Express. Apart from the cantonment stories, nature, and environment are recurring themes in his writing.

Dr Surya Kaladhar - Homecoming

Dr M. Surya Kaladhar is Ph.D holder and has 3 decades of experience in teaching field. She is bestowed with meritorious "Best Teachers Award" by Government of Andhra Pradesh in September 2000 and held many posts like HOD, in Kasturba Gandhi College, and coordinator for distance education in Osmania University and Dr. B. R. Ambedkar open University.

Saheli Banerji - He is a Soldier

Saheli Banerji is from Kolkata, she is Lecturer in English. For Saheli writing has been always her passion. Now she has taken up writing as her full-time profession. Apart from being a poet and short stories writer she is a professional novelist too.

Some of her work include Pools of Blood, Murder of the king, Miscellany of Odes (Paperback on Amazon), Rhythms of Life (Paperback on Amazon) etc. Her new book "Zingedi Ek Eheshas" is in publication process. You can check out her work @ www.gobuSpeaks.com/blog

Swapnil Saurav - Ghosts in the Walls

Swapnil Saurav grew up in Hyderabad and is a Data Scientist by profession. He started writing Technology books in the year 2013 and subsequently Friction stories in 2018. He writes about common people and describes things which can happen in anybody's life. He writes prose in English and poetry in Hindi. His book on Data Science & Machine Learning using Python is latest addition to his Tech series collection. His complete work can be found at: https://amazon.com/author/swapnil

EDITOR

Kumari Smriti - Editor

Smriti, an engineer by habit, a manager by profession, a teacher by interest and an avid reader by hobby. Being amongst writers and readers gives me a sense of belonging to the alternate world created by writing. Editing stories is my way of being exploring this world of imaginations.

DESIGNER

Aniruddh Vaidya - Cover Design

Aniruddh Vaidya is an engineer by profession and is currently heading operations at a EdTech startup in Hyderabad. He has parallelly managed marketing, sales and operation teams and created extensive collateral materials in the past for the startups he worked. For Aniruddh designing is more of a hobby and he tries to get his ideas in the form of designs. Photography is also one of his passions, in his free time you will find him clicking photos from his DSLR. He likes nature and portrait photography.

PUBLISHER

Eka Publishers

Eka is a Hyderabad based publishing house owned and run by group of experts like Authors, Editors and Designers. We firmly believe that a book is a result of lot of hard work and effort put by the authors and so the publishing should be easy and effortless. Our experts work overtime to bring best quality of work to the public domain. We have adopted a mid-path between traditional (where it's almost impossible to get published) and self (where they charge very high cost for publication) publishing. We offer plethora of services. We put our effort in book promotion through variety of channels so that out authors get good visibility. You can reach out to us at: ekapresshyderabad@gmail.com or publish@ekapress.org

Visit the website at: www.ekapress.org
Whatsapp/Phone: +91 8008101590

www.ingramcontent.com/pod-product-compliance
Lightning Source LLC
Chambersburg PA
CBHW061238140726
47998CB00006B/2028